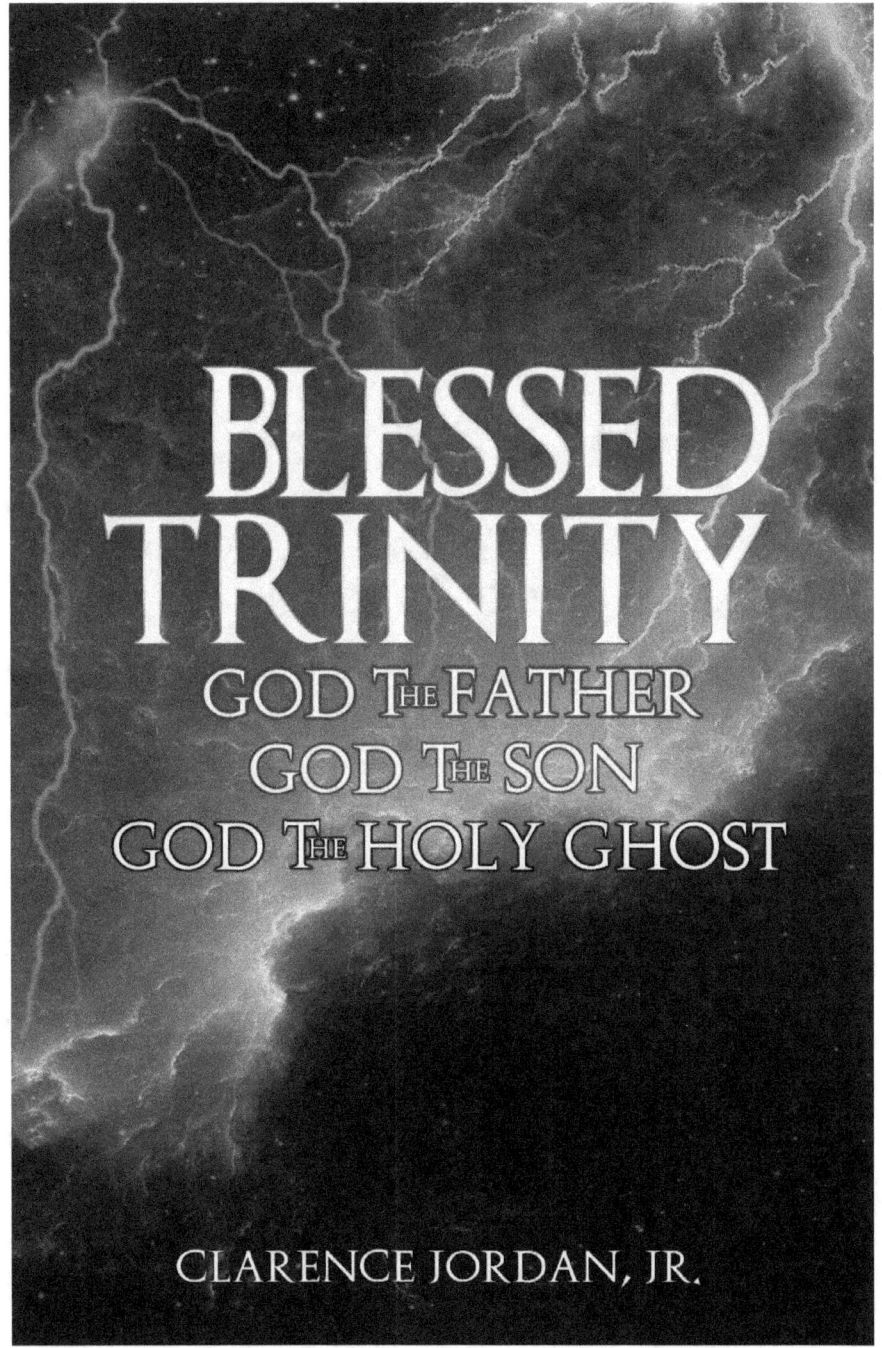

Clarence Jordan, Jr.

BLESSED TRINITY:
God The Father
God The Son
God The Holy Ghost

Clarence Jordan, Jr.

Pearly Gates Publishing, LLC, Houston, Texas

Blessed Trinity

Blessed Trinity:
God The Father, God The Son, God The Holy Ghost

Copyright © 2018
Clarence Jordan, Jr.

All Rights Reserved.
No portion of the publication may be reproduced, stored in any electronic system, or transmitted in any form or by any means (electronic, mechanical, photocopy, recording, or otherwise) without written permission from the publisher. Brief quotations may be used in literary reviews.

ISBN 13: 978-1-947445-17-8
Library of Congress Control Number: 2018941962

Scripture references are used with permission from
Zondervan via Biblegateway.com.
Public Domain.

Printed in the United States of America.

For information and bulk ordering, contact:
Pearly Gates Publishing, LLC
Angela Edwards, CEO
P.O. Box 62287
Houston, TX 77205
BestSeller@PearlyGatesPublishing.com

Clarence Jordan, Jr.

DEDICATIONS

First and foremost, I dedicate this book to
God the Father,
God the Son,
and **God the Holy Ghost.**
Because of Your indescribable, inconceivable love for me, you saved me from my sins and filled me with Your precious gift of the Holy Ghost. Without You in my life, I would have never made it. You inspired me to write this book to encourage the body of Christ and to win lost souls for the Kingdom of God.
For that, I am grateful.

In memoriam of my late father,
Elder Clarence Jordan, Sr.,
who is forever in Heaven with God.
He would be so well-pleased with such a remarkable composition written by his oldest son.
I love and miss you very much, Dad.

In memoriam of my late aunt,
Evangelist and First Lady Eartha Bell Evans,
who is forever in Heaven with God.
She was instrumental in leading me to Christ. She would be so happy for my success as an accomplished book author.
I love you and miss you very much, Auntie.

ACKNOWLEDGEMENTS

To God be the glory for all He has done.

To my Mother, Bunnia Lee Jordan: Thank you so much for your love, support, encouragement, and prayers. I love you, Mom, very much.

To my Siblings Earline Jordan, Matthew & Tabetha Jordan, and Darelle & Jannet Williams: Thank you all for your love, support, encouragement, and prayers. I love you all very much.

To Bishop Willie A. Jenkins, Sr., my former Pastor of Greater Law Memorial Church of God in Christ in Houston, Texas: You are a great gospel preacher, a great man of God, and a great humanitarian. Thank you for your labor of love towards me and your encouragement, support, and prayers. Your kindness will never be forgotten. My beloved Pastor, mentor, adopted father, and friend: I love you very much.

To Michael and Dareen Butler: Thank you for your recommendation, prayers, and support. I love you both very much.

To Angela R. Edwards, CEO & Editor-in-Chief of Pearly Gates Publishing, LLC: Thank you for your professionalism, expertise, advice, endorsement, and patience throughout this whole publication. Your editing work is extraordinary and I am appreciative.

Clarence Jordan, Jr.

To Pearly Gates Publishing, LLC's on-staff Graphic Designer: Thank you for your incredible hard work and expertise in creating and designing the book cover for publication.

Clarence Jordan, Jr.

TABLE OF CONTENTS

DEDICATIONS vi
ACKNOWLEDGEMENTS vii
INTRODUCTION 1
   WHO IS GOD? 1
CHAPTER 1: God is a Triune Being 6
CHAPTER 2: Attributes of God 7
CHAPTER 3: Origin of God 8
CHAPTER 4: God the FATHER 14
CHAPTER 5: Abba Father 16
CHAPTER 6: A Loving Father 19
CHAPTER 7: God the Father's Love 21
     PHILEO 21
     EROS 21
     STORGE 22
     AGAPE 22
CHAPTER 8: God the Son 28
CHAPTER 9: Wisdom Calling 30
CHAPTER 10: Jesus 33
CHAPTER 11: Christ — The Great Intercessor 35
     THE FIRST ATTEMPT ON JESUS' LIFE 36
     THE SECOND ATTEMPT ON JESUS' LIFE 36
     THE THIRD ATTEMPT ON JESUS' LIFE 36
     THE FOURTH ATTEMPT ON JESUS' LIFE 36
     THE FIFTH ATTEMPT ON JESUS' LIFE 37
     THE SIXTH ATTEMPT ON JESUS' LIFE 37

CHAPTER 12: Jesus Preaches in Hell 59
CHAPTER 13: Jesus' Resurrection 60
CHAPTER 14: SPECIAL NOTE 66
CHAPTER 15: God the Holy Ghost 69
    THE HOLY GHOST AS THE AUTHOR OF HOLY SCRIPTURES 70
    THE HOLY GHOST AS THE COMFORTER 71
    THE HOLY GHOST AS THE SPIRIT OF TRUTH 72
    THE HOLY GHOST AS THE SEALER 73
    THE HOLY GHOST AS THE REVEALER 74
    THE HOLY GHOST AS THE INDWELLER OF BELIEVERS 75
    THE HOLY GHOST AS THE SPIRIT OF LIFE 77
    THE HOLY GHOST AS THE TEACHER 78
CHAPTER 16: FIVE SYMBOLS OF THE HOLY GHOST 79
    DOVE 79
    FIRE 79
    OIL 80
    WATER 81
    WIND 82
CONCLUSION 83
INVITATION TO CHRISTIAN DISCIPLESHIP 84
1 JOHN 1:9 - JOURNALING 86
CLOSING PRAYER 94

Blessed Trinity

Clarence Jordan, Jr.

INTRODUCTION

WHO IS GOD?

Many people have asked this question because they are searching for the truth. Their heart yearns for the right answers to their unsolved mystery. There has been a myriad of people who have addressed this question to many different religious leaders.

There have been many people who left church services with a greater understanding of who God is, while others remain uncertain and puzzled about His existence. There are others, such as atheists, who reject religious belief and believes there is no God. As well, there are religions out there that contradict who God is and what He expects out of true Christianity.

"They have a form of godliness but denying the power."
2 Timothy 3:5

"They" profess to be Christians, but their ungodly behavior reveals hypocrisy. In other words, "they" are pretending to be someone they are not. "They" possess no evidence of the power of God in their lives. Even though there may be reformation (religion), there is not manifestation of regeneration (spiritual rebirth).

Mythology is the science or study of myths. Myths are also stories, tales, or legends that are not real. Books have been written by mythologists about gods such as Odin, a chief deity and god of art, culture, war, and the dead. There is also Thor, the son of Odin, who is the god of thunder, war, and strength. His weapon is the 'magic hammer'. Odin and Thor were the myth of the medieval Scandinavian people who were called "Norsemen" or "Vikings". Let's not forget about Zeus, a chief deity and sky and thunder god! Also, Hercules the son of Zeus, famous for his strength and courage, a god in human flesh. Zeus and Hercules were myths of the Greek and Roman people.

Hollywood has brought these imaginary characters to the big screen by either the movies or television. Hollywood has generated millions of dollars because of the audiences that showed up at the box office desiring to watch actors and actresses portray fictional characters with fictional powers. The emphasis and hype on promoting entertainment and entertainers today has become a 'god' to many people. Entertainers such as singers, dancers, comedians, actors, and actresses are called "Icons" in the entertainment industry. Because of their professional career as an entertainer, they are treated by their fans as "gods and goddesses".

Audiences are captivated by movies and television shows that exhibit carnage, horror, profanity, and sexuality. More and more demonic movies are being released every year that display Ouija Boards, witchcraft, seances, satanic rituals, and psychics conjuring up demons. Pornography, adultery, fornication, and homosexuality have become popular in Hollywood mainstream. Sinful, wicked behaviors have been fully-embraced by society as a whole. It is disgraceful to see men French kissing men and women French kissing women at the box office, on cable television, and now, even network television. This is attributed to the influence of Satan's power at work, blinding the minds of unbelievers (2 Corinthians 4:4). According to the Bible, pornography, adultery, fornication, and homosexuality are absolutely wrong (Hebrews 13:4; Ezekiel 43:9; Revelation 17:1-2; Genesis 19:13; and Romans 1:25-32).

Throughout the Bible—from Genesis to Revelation—the children of Israel would turn from the True and Living God and worship false gods. I'm reminded of the Prophet Elijah who met with Ahab, the wicked King of the Northern Kingdom of Israel, which was arranged by Obadiah (1 Kings 18:14-16). When Ahab finally approached Elijah, the dialogue begins with Ahab falsely accusing Elijah of being a troublemaker to Israel (1 Kings 18:17). Elijah turns the tables on King Ahab and rebukes him for forsaking the commandments of God, following after a false god, and causing Israel to commit idolatry (1 Kings 18:18). So, Elijah the Prophet commanded King Ahab to assemble all the children of Israel, the 450 prophets of Baal, and the 400 prophets of Asherah at Mount Carmel (1 Kings 18:19-20). Well, everyone shows up…except the 400 prophets of Asherah.

Elijah began to publicly address the people about their indecision to choose between the Lord God or Baal the false god. "Since you are unable to decide, I am issuing a contest against the 450 prophets of Baal to end this conflict" (1 Kings 18:21-22). "The God that answers by fire will be acknowledged as the True and Living God" (1 Kings 18:24).

Each contestant was given one bull to place on the kindling wood. Elijah represented the Lord God. The 450 prophets represented Baal the false god. Elijah allowed the 450 prophets to call upon their god first. The prophets yelled out to their god from morning to noon, but there was no answer. So, they then jumped upon the altar which had been prepared. At noon, Elijah ridiculed them. That caused them to yell out even louder as they cut themselves with knives and lancets, causing their blood to pour out of their flesh (1 Kings 18:26-28). By this time, noonday had past. The prophets of Baal prophesied until the time of the evening sacrifice. Still, there was no answer. The prophets of Baal really stood out as idiots! Eventually, the focus and attention they had received while calling on their false god came to an end (1 Kings 18:29).

When it was Elijah's turn to call upon his God, he called the people to come close to him and repaired the altar that had been broken down by the prophets (1 Kings 18:30). Elijah also took 12 stones, which represented the 12 tribes of Israel (1 Kings 18:31) and used the stones to build an altar in dedication to the Lord God (1 Kings 18:32). He made sure that all possibilities of the altar catching fire any other way other than by GOD would be eliminated. The miraculous Lord God would be the ONLY way. Elijah put the wood in order and cut the bull into fragments. He then laid the bull on the wood. He then commanded that four barrels be filled with water and poured onto both the bull AND the wood. Elijah went on to command that the people in charge of the pouring repeat the process a second AND third time so that the altar and trench were completely saturated with water (1 Kings 18:33-35).

Elijah then prayed to the Lord God that He would reveal Himself and send fire from Heaven. Towards the closing of his prayer, he petitioned God on behalf of the children of Israel and acknowledged the Lord God as the True and Living God. Elijah also acknowledged God for bringing restoration back to Israel. Immediately, the Lord God caused fire to descend from Heaven, consuming the sacrificial bull, the wood, the stones, the dust, and the water in the trench around the altar (1 Kings 18:36-38).

NOTE: There is NO scientific explanation for fire descending from Heaven and consuming everything that was upon and below the altar. This was purely an **EXCEEDINGLY, AWESOME ACT OF GOD!**

So, who is this God that causes fire to fall from Heaven? He is certainly not a myth or fairytale. God is very real, indeed! He is the "Ancient of Days" (Daniel 7:9). In other words, He has existed before time—days, weeks, months, and years—was ever established. You must understand that God is before there ever was (Hebrews 11:6). He has always existed throughout all eternity (Psalm 90:2). He is the Supreme Being who created and controls the cosmos. This is a phenomenon which boggles the human mind. How can a God create the whole universe out of nothing? The truth of the matter is this:

BY HIS INFINITE WISDOM AND INFINITE POWER!

It is an exceedingly great privilege and an exceedingly great honor to share with you the True and Living God!

CHAPTER 1: God is a Triune Being

Within the Godhead, there consists three divine personalities:

- ❖ God the Father
- ❖ God the Son
- ❖ God the Holy Ghost

These three entities are the Blessed Trinity — the union of three divine persons in one Godhead (1 John 5:7).

"God is a Spirit: and they that worship Him must worship Him in spirit and in truth."
John 4:24

CHAPTER 2: Attributes of God

God is Omnipotent, meaning He is All-Powerful or Almighty, possessing unlimited power and authority (Revelation 19:6). There is no angel, devil, demon, man, or any other power that can resist the power of God. God's power is irresistible and unstoppable. He is and always will be undefeated.

God is Omniscient, meaning He is All-Knowing. Every strand of hair on our heads is numbered, and God knows the number of hairs we have (Matthew 10:30). God also knows our past, present, and future. In other words, He knows everything. NOTHING is hidden from Him. From His throne, He knows everything about everyone…ALL the time (Psalm 33:13-15).

God is Omnipresent, meaning He is always present—everywhere at all times. He is not limited or restricted to one location at a time. He is EVERYWHERE…at the same time (Psalm 139:8).

God is Infallible, meaning He is incapable of making mistakes or being wrong (Genesis 18:1-33). He is perfect in ALL His ways. There are no flaws in Him (Psalm 18:30).

God is Unchangeable in His nature, which consists of His gifts, grace, love, mercy, perfections, promises, and purposes. God remains the same yesterday, today, and forever (Hebrews 13:8).

CHAPTER 3: Origin of God

Even though I have never been asked the following questions, I am sure many people have asked others:

Where did God come from?

Does He have a father and mother?

Who created God?

How did He come into existence?

The truth is that God did not "come" from anywhere; neither was He created "by" anyone. He does not have a father or mother. He was not created by anyone nor anything. He has no beginning or ending. No predecessor existed before Him; neither will there be a successor after Him. God is simultaneously past, present, and future (Revelation 1:8). He is the architect of Heaven and earth (Genesis 1:1).

The Bible mentions the existence of three Heavens. The first Heaven is the atmosphere above us, which is the blue sky (Genesis 1:6-8). The second is called the 'Solar' or 'Stellar Heaven', which is the sun, moon, stars, and planets (Genesis 1:3-5). The third Heaven is the highest Heaven where God's throne is. This is the place He created for Himself in which to reside (2 Corinthians 12:2). Also residing in the third Heaven are Heavenly Hosts called angels or angelic beings. Before earth was created by God, angels were created by Him to give unceasing worship and praise to Him forever and ever (Revelation 4:8-9). Angels accompanied God in the creation of earth. The Bible says that the morning stars sang together, and all the sons of God shouted for joy (Job 38:7).

Saints who die in Christ will be escorted by angels to Heaven (if that is their destination) (Luke 16:19-31). After death, there is judgment (Hebrews 9:27). We will all appear before the Judgment Seat of Christ, at which time everyone will receive either reward or punishment—things that hinge upon whether we lived to please or reject Christ during our earthly life. In other words, if we die without Christ, our souls will suffer eternal damnation...FOREVER. If we die in Christ, we will live forever in Heaven (2 Corinthians 5:10).

Angels are also ministering spirits, dispatched by God Almighty to minister to human beings who are entitled to salvation (Hebrews 1:14). Angels also have the power or ability to morph into a human being. We must never neglect the opportunity to entertain or show benevolence to a stranger, who could very well be an unsuspecting angel (Hebrews 13:2).

The cosmos or universe is the total completion of God's creation existing on planet earth today. God is the Creator and Sustainer of the whole universe (Psalm 146:5-9).

I am prayerful that anthropologists, atheists, evolutionists, and scientists will respectively understand that GOD created man in His image and in His likeness. GOD has given man power and authority over all the earth (Genesis 1:26-28). The truth of the matter is that man has never "evolved" from an ape. That is a lie straight from the pit of Hell!

Clarence Jordan, Jr.

Humans are not primates and will never be. Examples of primates are baboons, monkeys, chimpanzees, orangutans, gorillas, and lemurs. God did not create primates in His likeness or image. Primates do not possess the God-given intelligence of mankind.

I have seen documentaries about primates. I have learned that chimpanzees and orangutans posses the strength of six men and that gorillas possess the strength of 20 men. Now, if these primates possessed the intelligence of man, clearly man would not be dominating the earth. My point here is that primates have no clue just how strong they are. Have you ever heard of any primates escaping from the zoo by using a pick or some other object to unlock the door of their cage? How about the use of dental floss to make their great escape from the zoo? The answer to both questions is a resounding "NO!"

On June 29, 1994, a prisoner escaped from the South Central Regional Jail's recreation yard in Charleston, West Virginia by scaling an 18-foot wall. He used a rope made from dental floss that was purchased through the jail's store. Understand here that primates do not possess the ingenuity and creativity to build things. The man's escape from prison didn't happen overnight; it was a well-thought-out plan that had been in motion for years. The inmate braided the dental floss to the thickness of a telephone cord. (Who would have ever thought of dental floss as a means of escape from prison?) It certainly wasn't a primate! A primate does not possess the skills that have been exclusively reserved for mankind. God has blessed us with those gifts!

So, just who IS this MAGNIFICENT GOD? Let's explore the Triune God in the following chapters!

Clarence Jordan, Jr.

GOD THE FATHER

CHAPTER 4: God the FATHER

God the FATHER is the first person and chief head of the Godhead. He is also the Father of all creation, meaning He is the Father of the universe. Not only is He the Author and Creator of all things, He is also the source of all creation, life, and energy, too. He is described as a 'Jasper and Sardine Stone, sitting upon His throne in majesty and splendor' (Revelation 4:3).

God the Father said, "Let us create man in our image and likeness" (Genesis 1:26). Mankind was placed on earth as God's representative and is similar to Him in certain ways. Just as God is a Triune being (Father, Word, and the Holy Ghost), man is a tripartite being (spirit, water, and blood) (1 John 5:7-8). Also, man is spirit, soul, and body (1 Thessalonians 5:23).

Like God, man has the intellect to know right from wrong, the ability to communicate with others and reason or understand, and the power of thought and tendency to get emotional. God has given man sovereignty to subdue the earth (Genesis 1:28). God has also commanded mankind to be fruitful and multiply. I believe this means more than just having children. It also encompasses ministry. As angels worship God in Heaven, man is commanded to worship God in the earth. Jesus told the woman at the well that God is a Spirit; and they that worship Him must worship Him in spirit and in truth (John 4:24). When we worship God, we don't worship Him in order to receive gifts from Him. Rather, we worship God just for who He is.

God is a jealous God. He commands us to worship no other gods but Him. God has a right to be jealous when we worship other gods because HE is the Creator of mankind!

"For thou shalt worship no other god;
for the LORD, whose name is jealous, is a jealous God."
(Exodus 34:14)

CHAPTER 5: Abba Father

"Abba" is an intimate term for God as Father (in the New Testament). The word Abba is an Aramaic word that would most closely be translated as "Daddy". This is commonly used today by children who address their fathers. It signifies the close, intimate relationship of a father with his child, as well as a young child placing confidence in his "daddy". We are God the Father's creation and under His authority and Lordship, the judge of all mankind in the earth. You must understand that not all people are sons and daughters of God.

Jesus said that if you are unsaved, you belong to your "father the devil" because he fills you with his wickedness.

"Ye are of your father the devil, and the lusts of your father ye will do. He was a murderer from the beginning, and abode not in the truth, because there is no truth in him. When he speaketh a lie, he speaketh of his own: for he is a liar and the father of it."
(John 8:44)

God the Father is our "Dear Father". Just as children have a relationship with their earthly father, we, as Christians, have a relationship with our Heavenly Father who loves us unconditionally. It is God the Father's good pleasure to give us the Kingdom (Luke 12:32).

"We are heirs of God the Father, and joint-heirs with Christ Jesus."
(Romans 8:17)

We cannot have a relationship with God the Father unless we've been granted access by the Son. Jesus made it clear that He is the Way, the Truth, and the Life: NO MAN comes to the Father but by Him (John 14:6).

We can approach the throne of grace in times of need with confidence and courage in the High Priest seated at the right hand of God the Father, interceding for us as a power of attorney (Hebrews 4:16).

God the Father's eternal purpose, which was fulfilled in His Son Jesus Christ our Lord, was the plan of salvation for all humanity (Ephesians 3:11).

We now have the unlimited privilege of entering into God the Father's presence at any time, with full confidence and boldness of being heard and without any fear of being rebuked or turned away (Ephesians 3:12).

Blessed by God, which hath not turned away my prayer, nor His mercy from me (Psalm 66:20).

Paul desired that the Ephesians not be discouraged because of his persecution and incarceration in Rome for preaching the gospel. He was delighted to endure tribulations for the sake of his mission to the Gentiles. He wanted the Ephesians to be well-pleased, knowing that he was counted worthy to suffer for the Lord Christ Jesus. Paul wanted the Ephesians to rejoice rather than be discouraged by his sufferings, which was a benefit to them (Ephesians 3:12-13). I believe God granted the Apostle Paul the grace of fortitude. His endurance, perseverance, and determination of mind enabled him to encounter persecution, danger, affliction, and much adversity with courage. The discouragement of the Ephesians was towards Paul's suffering, which caused him to pray for their spiritual strength through God the Father (Ephesians 3:14).

God the Father is the Head Author and Creator of all angelic beings in Heaven and all of mankind on the earth (Ephesians 3:15). All angelic beings, as well as all the redeemed on the earth, acknowledges God the Father as the Head of the royal family.

"For ye are all the children of God by faith in Christ Jesus."
Galatians 3:26

CHAPTER 6: A Loving Father

We are fearfully and wonderfully made by God (Psalm 139:14). Notice the Psalmist David was exploring God's omnipotent power in creating mankind, His prized possession.

The process of an infant in his/her mother's womb starts with the chromosomes or DNA that is passed from the parents to the offspring. If the chromosomes are 'XY', the parents will have a son. If the chromosomes are 'XX', the parents will have a daughter. The characteristics of the child are developed in the color of his/her skin, eyes, and hair, the shape of his/her facial features, and even the natural talents or skills he/she will have. God knew us before we were formed in our mother's womb and sanctified us for His use (Jeremiah 1:5).

Our Heavenly Father loves us so much that He honors us as His sons and daughters. And for that reason, the world does not recognize us; nor did they recognize Jesus who testified of His Father in Heaven (1 John 3:1).

Jesus said that He provides evidence of Himself and the Father who sent Him provides evidence of Him as well (John 8:18).

God the Father's voice was heard after John had baptized Jesus, declaring His blessings and recognition to His Only Begotten Son (Matthew 3:17). God the Father's voice was heard again out of a cloud which had overshadowed Peter, James, and John while they witnessed the transfiguration of Jesus on the mountain. The Father from Heaven declared that this is His Beloved Son, in whom He is well pleased; listen to

Him (Matthew 17:5). Peter, James, and John witnessed a divine visitation of the presence of God the Father giving honor and glory to Jesus by His resounding voice from Heaven, acknowledging, "This is my Beloved Son, in whom I am well pleased" (2 Peter 1:17-18). The inner circle were eye witnesses to the change of appearance in Christ Jesus and the voice of God the Father from Heaven.

Jesus wanted God the Father's name to be glorified, rather than being saved from the cross. Immediately, God the Father's voice was heard from Heaven. Some people that were nearby mistakenly thought it was thunder. Others thought an angel had spoke to Him. There are always non-spiritual people making wrong assessments on supernatural events they do not understand (John 12:28-29).

Non-believers are always rejecting the miracles of God. They discredit the supernatural influence of Heaven as some natural common law. God defies all natural laws. He is not confined, subjected, nor bound by the force of gravity as human beings are.

GOD'S POWER, KNOWLEDGE, AND PRESENCE ARE UNLIMITED! He is everywhere at the same time.

He is the Blessed Trinity — a Spirit-being who reigns supreme forever.

CHAPTER 7: God the Father's Love

God the Father's love for humanity is a love that is immeasurable. His love for us never runs out. There are different kinds of love, but which love emerges as GOD'S love?

PHILEO

Phileo is a Greek word which means "brotherly love between close friends."

"A man that hath friends must shew himself friendly; and there is a friend that sticketh closer than a brother."
(Proverbs 18:24)

Is Phileo the only kind of love our Heavenly Father shows to us all? **No!**

EROS

Eros is a Greek word which means "romantic or intimate love that involves a physical, sexual love found between a man and woman within the confines of marriage."

"Let the husband render unto the wife due benevolence; and likewise, also the wife unto the husband."
(1 Corinthians 7:3)

"The wife hath not power of her own body, but the husband; and likewise also, the husband hath not power of his own body, but the wife."
(1 Corinthians 7:4)

As Christians in Christ Jesus, we have an intimate relationship with God. Is Eros the kind of love God renders to us? **No!**

STORGE

Storge is a Greek word which is "a love for the family." Loving your family is important. Loving your earthy father, mother, your siblings, and other relatives is wonderful!

> "Now, therefore, ye are no more strangers and foreigners, but fellow citizens with the saints, and of the household of God."
> (Ephesians 2:19)

Is Storge the only kind of love God gives? **No!**

AGAPE

Agape love is the highest form of love, which is unconditional and universal brotherly love towards all ethnicities. This is the kind of love that our Heavenly Father shows to us all.

> "God the Father's love for mankind was demonstrated towards us, that while we were yet sinners, Christ died for us."
> (Romans 5:8)

> "Father God is merciful to our unrighteousness, our sins, and our iniquities. He will remember them no more."
> (Hebrews 8:12)

God's love takes precedence over any spiritual gifts that He gives to us (1 Corinthians 13:1-2).

God's love even takes precedence over us, giving all our goods to feed the poor, and giving our body to be a sacrifice. If it is not done in the spirit of love, it will not profit or benefit you (1 Corinthians 13:3).

God's love is longsuffering and is kind. Love does not encourage envy or jealousy. God's love does not promote showmanship, boasting, or self-centeredness (1 Corinthians 13:4).

God's love does not cause improper manner; nor does it attempt to pursue its own selfish gain. God's love is not easily stimulated by reactions or emotions when confronted by unwelcomed insults. God's love is never vindictive; neither does He retaliate against any enemy who has done Him wrong (1 Corinthians 13:5).

The Apostle Paul's letter to the Roman church was not to recompense or repay any man evil for evil, but to show honesty to all men. Paul also goes on to say, "With all that is in our being as a Christian, live peaceably with all men" (Romans 12:17-18).

God's love causes His sons and daughters to love peace, make peace, and be at peace (Proverbs 16:7).

The God of Peace shall crush Satan under our feet soon (Romans 16:20).

Paul warns against getting revenge or avenging someone who has purposely done you wrong. Vengeance is

God's prerogative. He will settle the matter at the appointed time and execute justice to wrongdoers (Romans 12:19).

The next verse takes you into the deep sea of benevolence of love and peace in dealing with your enemy.

Paul says if your enemy is hungry, feed him; if he is thirsty, give him something to drink. When you show acts of kindness to your enemy, you are heaping coals of fire on his head (Romans 12:20).

What does 'heaping coals of fire on his head' mean? I'm glad you asked that question!

This simply means to make your enemies ashamed of their hostility towards you by surprising them with unconventional or out-of-the-ordinary kindness!

The last exhortation Paul shares with the Roman church in this chapter is not to render evil for evil but overcome evil by doing good (Romans 12:21).

Faith, hope, and love are three spiritual principles that go hand-in-hand in this present age. They are vital to every spirit-filled Christian's life. They are superior to the gifts of the Spirit. In the age to come, faith and hope will eventually vanish. In other words, they will be no more. We will be with God the Father and God the Son and God the Holy Ghost — FOREVER! God will wipe away all our tears. Death shall be no more; neither sorrow or crying; neither will there be any more pain: previous things on earth are passed away (Revelation 21:3-4).

Blessed Trinity

"But love shall remain in the age to come throughout all eternity; because God is love."
1 John 4:8

Clarence Jordan, Jr.

GOD THE SON

CHAPTER 8: God the Son

God the Son exists throughout all eternity as an equal member of the Godhead. God the Son has always coexisted with God the Father. God the Son is the active agent that caused creation to be, for by Him were all things created that are in Heaven, and that are in the earth, visible and invisible whether they be thrones, or dominions, or principalities, or powers; all things were created by Him and for Him (Colossians 1:16).

In the New Testament, the writer Apostle John declares the pre-existence of God the Son as the Living Word of God. The Greek word "Logos", which means 'living word', caused the cosmos or universe to be manifested. John also states that the Living Word of God (or Son of God) was with God the Father, and that He Himself is God and Creator of all things (John 1:1-3). The Living Word, which is Jesus Christ, is without beginning. He is from everlasting to everlasting (Proverbs 8:23).

Even though God the Father and God the Son are One, God the Son's eternal existence and His personality are distinct from that of God the Father (Revelation 4:3; 5:6). Jesus, the Son of God, is the Sustainer and Source of life. He is the source of physical and spiritual life. When we were born into this world, we received physical life. When we are born again, we receive spiritual life. Both come from Him (John 1:4).

Jesus is the Light of the World! Those who choose to live for Christ are given guidance and direction by Him. Sin caused man to be in darkness. Man did not realize who Jesus really was or why he came to earth. Jesus said that he that believeth on Him is not condemned; but he that believeth not is condemned already because he has not believed in the name of the only Begotten Son of God. Light exposes darkness and uncovers the sinfulness and shame of the sinner. That is why men love darkness—because their actions are evil (John 3:18-19).

The Book of Revelation presents our Lord Jesus Christ as both "Lamb" and "Lion". As the Lamb of God, He is the ultimate sacrificial one, taking away the sins of the world. As the Lion, He is the ultimate judge of the saints and sinners.

Every human being has an appointment with death, but after death comes judgment (Hebrews 9:27).

Judgment will begin with the saints of God. If judgment begins with us first, what will be the future of those who reject the Gospel of Jesus Christ? If the righteous can barely make it to Heaven, then what will happen to the sinner and ungodly person (1 Peter 4:17-18)?

CHAPTER 9: Wisdom Calling

"For whoso findeth me findeth life and shall obtain favour of the Lord. But he that sinneth against me wrongeth his own soul: all they that hate Me love death."
(Proverbs 8:35-36)

This is an eternal invitation from Jesus, the Son of God. He is inviting all who will believe on His name to accept Him as Lord and Savior. When we receive Him into our life, we are granted eternal life and access to the blessings of the Lord.

"He that believeth on the Son hath everlasting life: and he that believeth not on the Son shall not see life; but the wrath of God abideth on him."
(John 3:36)

You must believe that Jesus died on the cross for your sins and repent, for the Kingdom of God is at hand. Repent means to feel such regret or dissatisfaction of wrongdoing that you become godly sorrowful for the sins you committed against God, which causes you to have a change of mind. However, if we refuse such an offer and reject Christ, we are in danger of Hell and the Lake of Fire and Brimstone.

Beloved, when you stand before God the Son, will YOUR name be found written in the Lamb's Book of Life?

If your name is absent from the Lamb's Book of Life, you will suffer torment in Hell and, eventually, be cast into the Lake of Fire (Revelation 20:15). This is considered the second death.

REMEMBER THIS! NO COMFORT! NO PEACE! NO REST FOR ALL OF ETERNITY!

Jesus was made a little lower than the angels exclusively for 33 years of His earthly ministry. He was commissioned to suffer and die for sinners, crowned with glory and honor; that He, by the grace of God, should taste death for every human being (Hebrews 2:9).

Adam's transgression caused the nature of mankind to be sinful (Romans 5:12). Anyone who willfully sins is of the devil. Sin originated in the heart of Lucifer (who is now called Satan or the devil). For this reason, the Son of God was manifested, to destroy the works of the devil (John 3:8). The power of death was taken away from Satan. He is a defeated foe. Death has been abolished; life and immortality has come to light through the gospel of Jesus Christ (2 Timothy 1:10).

The Father loves His Son. God the Father has given all things into God the Son's hands (John 3:35).

"Who being the brightness of His glory and express image of His person and upholding all things by the Word of His power, when He had by Himself purged our sins, sat down on the right hand of the Majesty on high."
(Hebrews 1:3)

Clarence Jordan, Jr.

In this scripture, we see Christology in a nutshell. The first part of the verse talks about the pre-existence of Christ and His relationship with His Father as Creator. The second part relates to the incarnation and crucifixion of Christ as the Purifier of our sins. The third part refers to the exaltation of Christ, the King of kings and Lord of lords, seated at the right hand of God the Father in Heaven, whose Kingdom shall never end.

Christ is directly related to the Father. The angels are not. Christ inherited the cosmos, and the angels are under His dominion. Christ is superior to angels, and the angels are subordinate to Him.

CHAPTER 10: Jesus

"The Angel Gabriel was sent from God to earth to a city of Galilee, named Nazareth, to a virgin who was engaged to be married to a man named Joseph."
Luke 1:26-27

"The Angel Gabriel declared to the virgin Mary that she is highly favored; that is chosen by God to conceive the Lord Jesus Christ."
Luke 1:28-31

The birth of Jesus was different from any human birth ever known to man. I am referring to the incarnation of Christ. Mary was impregnated by the Holy Ghost (Matthew 1:18).

It is a phenomenon to people who don't believe or understand the omnipotent power of God. It literally confounds the human mind because the human mind cannot conceive or process such a thing. Jesus, the Son of God, who is the second person of the Trinity, took on the form or nature of man. For He is the image of the invisible God, the firstborn of every creature (Colossians 1:15).

First of all, man has never seen the invisible God revealed in all His glory at ANY time because God's greatness is so awesome, man would literally fall dead in His presence (John 1:18; 5:37; Exodus 33:20). Moses was granted the privilege to see God's glory passing by while standing on a rock. Moses seen an appearance of God's back, and even THAT was too much (Exodus 33:21-23).

God is a Spirit and is, therefore, invisible. But in the person of Christ, God made Himself visible to mortal eyes. In that sense, the Lord Jesus is the image of the invisible God.

Philip asked Jesus to "show us [the disciples] the Father, and it will be enough." Jesus impassively corrected Philip. Philip was one of the first disciples to be called (John 1:43). Jesus simply told Philip, "You have been with Me for a long time and you still don't know Me?"

> *"He that has seen Me has seen the Father."*
> John 14:9

Jesus then asked Philip another question: "Do you believe that I am in the Father and the Father is in Me?" He was letting Philip know that He is the only one who is related to God the Father. Jesus is, indeed, God the Son. Jesus goes on to say, "The words I speak and the works I do are of the Father."

The "Last Supper" or "Communion" was in Jerusalem, which was held in the Upper Room (also known as a dining room). This second-story room was above the tomb of David. This was the place where Jesus had partaken the Last Supper with His disciples. As the disciples were eating, Jesus blessed the unleavened bread and wine. The bread represented His body (which was given for us). The wine represented His blood (which was shed for us) (Luke 22:19-20; John 12:32-33; 1 Corinthians 11:24-25).

CHAPTER 11: Christ—The Great Intercessor

In the Garden of Gethsemane, Jesus prayed to the Father to remove the cup of suffering from Him. Jesus humbly submits to the Father's will, knowing that He will drink of this bitter cup for the sake of humanity. Jesus uttered the following words: "Nevertheless, not My will, but Thine be done" (Luke 22:42). Jesus was in great agony. As He prayed more sincerely, His sweat was as great drops of blood falling to the ground (Luke 22:44).

I always thought that Christ feared having to endure punishment and death on a cross. The truth of the matter is this:

THAT IS WHY HE CAME.

So, it wasn't the fear of punishment and execution; it was the fear of being separated from His Father. God the Son has never been separated from His Father. Jesus knew that the sins of the world were being transferred to Him. Sin is what separated man from God. Sin carried a serious penalty, and that penalty was death (Romans 6:23).

"These words spake Jesus and lifted up His eyes to Heaven, and said,
"Father, the hour is come; glorify thy Son,
that thy Son also may glorify thee."
John 17:1

Jesus was Heavenward-bound. He was looking beyond suffering and death, perceiving the souls that shall be harvested into the Kingdom of God!

Jesus said, "Father, the hour is come." He knew that the moment in time had come on earth when He was to offer His life as a ransom for sinful man. There were five previous attempts on Jesus' life, but His hour had not come then. It wasn't until the sixth and final attempt that His mission was complete.

THE FIRST ATTEMPT ON JESUS' LIFE

King Herod wanted to kill Jesus when He was a child (Matthew 2:13).

THE SECOND ATTEMPT ON JESUS' LIFE

Satan brought Jesus to Jerusalem to the pinnacle of the Temple to commit suicide (Luke 4:9-12).

THE THIRD ATTEMPT ON JESUS' LIFE

Jesus was in His hometown, Nazareth, teaching in the synagogue. The people in the synagogue were extremely angry at His teachings, so they attempted to violently push Him head-first down over the cliff—but Jesus supernaturally walked through the crowd and departed from Nazareth (Luke 4:28-30).

THE FOURTH ATTEMPT ON JESUS' LIFE

During the third year of Jesus' public ministry, He was in Jerusalem teaching in the temple when disputation arose. Those "Jews who had believed in Him" debated with Him. In conclusion, Jesus told the audience, "Before Abraham was, I AM." This made His audience very angry. "So, they picked up stones to throw at him; but Jesus hid Himself and went out of the temple" (John 8:21-59).

THE FIFTH ATTEMPT ON JESUS' LIFE

During the Feast of the Dedication in the wintertime, which was in Jerusalem, Jesus was walking in the temple at a spot called 'Solomon's Porch'. The Jews surrounded Him, asking, "How long do you keep us in suspense? If you are Christ, just simply tell us." Jesus plainly told them, "I told you, but you do not believe the works that I do in My Father's name, they bear witness of Me" (John 10:22-25). Jesus concluded with these words: "If I do not the works of My Father, believe Me not. But if I do, though ye believe not Me, believe the works; that ye may know and believe that the Father is in Me, and I in Him" (John 10:37-38).

Jesus did not come to the earth for ambitious or selfish reasons. He was sent to do His Father's will. He told the Jews, "If I'm not here on divine assignment to do My Father's will, then don't believe Me. Believe the miracles of mercy and compassion that I do and believe that My Father and Me are One." So, out of anger, the Jews took action to apprehend Jesus, but He eluded them once again. It was not yet His time.

THE SIXTH ATTEMPT ON JESUS' LIFE

Please take note of this sixth attempt. Mankind was created on the sixth day, and the number six is man's number (Genesis 1:24-25). This was no coincident that His time had come to liberate humanity from sin.

King David prophesied in the Book of Psalms of a betrayer eating bread with Jesus (Psalms 41:9). Zechariah the Prophet inquired about his wages. His employed paid him 30 pieces of silver—a price of a slave—which he tossed into a potter in the house of the Lord. This was a prophecy of what the betrayer of Jesus would do in the New Testament Gospels (Zechariah 11:12-13).

Jesus made reference of the betrayer in Matthew and Mark's Gospel of the New Testament. Jesus knew that He had to fulfill every written prophesy for the redemption of humanity. "But woe to that man, that will betray the Son of Man. It would be better if he had never existed" (Matthew 26:24; Mark 14:21). In other words, he will not escape eternal punishment.

One of the most profound prayers Jesus ever prayed is recorded in the Gospel of John. In this scripture, Jesus tells His Father that He has kept all the disciples in His name. He guarded and protected them, and none of them is lost except for the son of perdition—the one who is doomed and destined for Hell for betraying Jesus (John 17:12).

This doomed man happened to be Judas Iscariot who betrayed Jesus with a kiss (at night) in the Garden of Gethsemane. This kiss identified Jesus as the man the Sanhedrin temple guards sought to apprehend.

Before Jesus was arrested, He asked them, "Whom seek ye?" In modern terminology: "Who are you looking for?" They responded by saying, "Jesus of Nazareth." When Jesus said, "I am He", they fell backwards to the ground. Now, you already

Blessed Trinity

know Jesus was absolutely too powerful for them. He used NO physical force or weapons—just three powerful words: "I AM HE" (John 18:4-6).

Please note that Jesus was protecting the disciples from being apprehended and harmed. So, Jesus asked them AGAIN, "Whom seek ye?" And their reply was, "Jesus of Nazareth." He had already told them He was the man they were looking for.

"If I'm the One, then let these men [disciples] go their way."
John 18:7-8

Jesus allowed the temple soldiers, captain, and officers of the Jews to capture and bind Him (John 18:12). He was then brought to Annas, a former High Priest. It is unclear why Jesus was brought to him first, rather than his son-in-law, Caiaphas, who was the High Priest at that time. This seems shady to me that protocol was broken and not properly followed. Jesus was put on trial for no reason at all. Those so-called religious leaders came up with this fabricated lie in order to "prove" Jesus guilty of blasphemy and heresy. They literally turned it into a religious trial against Jesus! Annas questioned Jesus about His disciples and His doctrine (teachings). Jesus replied by saying, "I spoke openly to the world; I taught in the synagogue and in the temple openly in the presence of the Jews. There was no secrecy. I had nothing to hide" (John 18:20). Jesus went on to say, "Why are you asking me these questions? Ask the religious leaders. They know because they heard me speak to them, and they know exactly what I said" (John 18:20).

After Jesus stopped speaking, one of the officials standing next to Him struck Jesus with the palm of his hand because he was offended by the way Jesus answered Annas (John 18:22). Jesus tells the official (in modern terminology), "If My testimony is false, you are a witness to My false testimony. Since My testimony is true, why, then, did you hit Me?" (John 18:23).

After the unnecessary line of questioning, Annas has Jesus bound and sent off to his son-in-law, Caiaphas the High Priest (John 18:24).

Peter denied that he knew or that he was a disciple of Jesus three times. Immediately, the rooster crowed twice. Peter remembered the words of Jesus and wept bitterly (Matthew 26:69-74; Mark 14:66-72; Luke 22:55-62; John 18:15-18, 25-27).

The Gospels of Matthew, Mark, and Luke explore the trial of Jesus in detail at the palace of the High Priest, Caiaphas, while John does not mention any details about the trial of Jesus or the false accusations that were presented against Him in the palace Caiaphas, who was the overseer of the trial.

Accompanying Caiaphas in this trial were the Scribes and Elders who questioned, mocked, spit on, blindfolded, and repeatedly and violently hit Jesus. All the while, they chanted, "Prophesy to the one that hit you!" Their plot was to kill Jesus (Matthew 26:59-68; Mark 14:55-65; Luke 22:63-65; John 18:24).

The Chief Priest held a conference with the Elders, Scribes, and the whole council. They bound Jesus and had Him carried away. Early in the morning on Passover Day, Jesus was led from the palace of Caiaphas to the Hall of Judgment and delivered to Pontius Pilate, the Governor, by a band of Roman soldiers. (The Sanhedrin Council would not enter into the palace of a Gentile. They felt it would prevent them from eating the Passover meal.) The Chief Priest, Scribes, and Elders highly regarded their religious customs and traditions — more importantly than the Son of God who was the ultimate Passover Lamb (Matthew 27:2; Mark 15:1; Luke 23:1; John 18:28-29).

Judas, the one who had betrayed Jesus, perceived that he was condemned to die and felt such deep regret within himself for the wrong he had done. Judas returned the 30 pieces of silver to the Chief Priests and Elders and told them that he has sinned and betrayed an innocent man. Their reply was (again in modern terminology), "Talk to the hand! This means nothing to us!" In desperation, Judas threw down the 30 pieces of silver in the temple, where only the Priest could go. He left out of the temple in a hurry with a guilty conscience…and committed suicide. It is concluded that Judas hanged himself from a tree. The rope or branch broke, and his body was thrown with great force over the edge of a cliff, causing it to be disemboweled (Matthew 27:3-5).

Pontius Pilate came outside the judgment hall to question the Sanhedrin Council about Jesus. "What accusation do you bring against this man?" Their reply was (in modern terminology), "We have already tried Him and found Him guilty. We just need you to announce the sentence." Pilate tried to avoid the responsibility of sentencing Jesus and tossed it back to the council. Pilate told them, "If you have found this man guilty, then judge Him according to your law." They responded by telling Pontius Pilate that it is not lawful for them to put any man to death. What the council was REALLY saying was, "We are not a free nation. We have been taken over by the Roman power. Civil authority has been stripped from our hands, and we no longer have authority to execute capital punishment on any man" (John 18:29-31).

Jesus had already predicted that He would be handed over to the Gentiles to be killed by being crucified on a cross (John 3:14; 8:28; 12:32, 34).

Pontius Pilate entered back in the judgment hall after speaking with the Sanhedrin Council to examine Jesus. Pontius asked Jesus, "Are you the King of the Jews?" (John 18:33). Jesus answered Pilate with His own question: "Did you learn this on your own or did others tell you about Me?" In other words, "Was it ever reported to you that I tried to conquer Roman power? Was it ever reported to you that I publicly announced Myself a King who would undermine Caesar's empire? The bottom line is: Did you investigate this charge on your own or are you going by hearsay information?" (John 18:34).

The, Pilate asked Jesus, "Am I a Jew?" What Pilate was really saying was that he is far too distinguished to be bothered with a local Jewish matter. "Even though your own Jewish people and Chief Priests have delivered you into my hands, there are no real charges against you, except for what the Sanhedrin Council has shared with me" (John 18:5). Jesus replied to Pilate's question with, "What hast thou done?" In other words, "What did you do?" Jesus continued: "My Kingdom is not of this earth. If My Kingdom was of the planet earth, then My servants would have fought and protected Me from being captured by the Jews" (John 18:36).

Pilate then asked Jesus, "Are you a King?" Jesus replied, "You say correctly that I am King."

Christ's Kingdom is about truth. This is why He was born. For this reason, He came to earth to bear witness to the truth: the truth about God the Father, Himself (God the Son), God the Holy Ghost, man, sin, salvation, and everything that is connected to the great doctrines of Christianity. Everyone who loves the truth hears the voice of Jesus. And this is how His empire grows (John 18:37).

Pontius Pilate was still questioning, "What is truth?" He could not perceive the words of Jesus. It was beyond his knowledge of thinking. He lacked understanding of truth and, consequently, could not receive truth because his heart was not open to accept the truth. After conversing with Jesus, Pilate stepped outside of the judgment hall and proclaimed to the Jewish people that he found no fault in Jesus (John 18:38).

Pilate acknowledged the custom of the Jewish Passover holiday by asking them, "Which man should I release unto you? Will it be Barabbas or the King of the Jews?"

Who was Barabbas? He was a robber, a rebel against Roman authority, and a murderer.

Jesus, in the reverse, was innocent of all charges against Him, but the religious leaders and Jewish people who were present wanted Barabbas released and Jesus to be crucified (John 18:40; Luke 23:18-19).

The decision was unanimous: Release Barabbas, a man clearly guilty of robbery, sedition, and murder.

Jesus was then taken by the Roman soldiers to a two-foot high whipping post where He was stripped naked, His hands were fastened tightly over His head to a metal ring, and His wrists were securely chained to the metal ring to restrain His body from movement. Most often, two Roman torturers were utilized to carry out this kind of punishment. Simultaneously, the torturers would lash the victim from both sides. The cat-o-nine-tails whip they used consisted of a handle (about 18" to 24" long) with a leather straps of about six to seven feet long. On the end of those nine strands were bits and pieces of metal, glass, wire, and jagged sheep bone. Every time the torturers struck Jesus with the cat-o-nine-tails whip, it would cut deeply through Jesus' skin and into His flesh, shredding His muscles and sinews. Then, the torturers would jerk back, pulling hard in order to tear whole pieces of human flesh from the victim's body.

Jesus' back, buttocks, back of legs, stomach, upper chest, and face were soon disfigured by the slashing blows from the whips. His back was so mutilated, His spine was actually exposed. Also, His bowels spilled out through the open wounds created by the whips. His veins, muscles, and sinews were exposed as well. If the whipping wasn't stopped, the slicing of the whips would eventually peel the skin off Jesus' body. The loss of blood caused Jesus' blood pressure to drop drastically. Because of the massive loss of bodily fluids, He experienced excruciating thirst, often fainting from the pain and eventually going into shock. His heartbeat became so irregular, He could have gone into cardiac arrest.

I want you to stop and think about something:

Jesus was severely, unimaginably, and horrifically beaten for the punishment of our sins (Isaiah 53:5; 1 Peter 2:24).

LET THAT SINK IN FOR A MOMENT…

After the severe beating, Jesus was then released from the whipping post. He had been humiliated, brutally and gruesomely scourged, and left laying in a pool of His own blood. He was trembling, extremely weak, dizzy, and queasy at the hands of the Roman torturers. They enjoyed every moment they tortured Jesus with those cat-o-nine-tails whips.

Jesus was then taken back into the Governor's palace. More Roman soldiers were summoned to keep Jesus under close surveillance. The soldiers then created a crown of thorns and placed it on Jesus' head. They firmly pressed the crown of thorns down upon His eyebrows, which caused Him excruciating pain. The sharp thorns caused blood to pour down from His head. The thorns represented the curse that sin brought to humanity (Genesis 3:14-19). Jesus bore this sin curse for us so that it would be removed forever from those who believe on His name.

After putting the crown of thorns upon Jesus' head, the Roman soldiers then clothed Him with a scarlet/purple robe.

The robe represented His royalty and sovereignty, even though they used it to mock Him.

I'm sure someone has a question mark in their mind concerning the scarlet/purple robe that was put on Jesus. In my mind, I can hear religious folks saying, "The Bible never indicated that the robe placed on Jesus by the Roman soldiers was scarlet/purple!" Allow me to clarify this matter so that you can receive a complete and perfect understanding of the point I am making.

Matthew's gospel described the robe as being scarlet, while Mark's and John's gospels described the robe as being purple (Matthew 27:28; Mark 15:17; John 19:2). Since two Gospel writers out of three specified that the robe Jesus was wearing was purple, one would conclude that purple was, indeed, the color.

Now, I'm also just as sure there are some religious folks who are saying, "That is correct, based upon what the Bible says about two or more people who are in agreement, then it is established" (Matthew 18:19-20). NOT SO! The Bible ALSO says, "Wisdom is the principal thing; therefore, get wisdom and with all your getting, get understanding" (Proverbs 4:7).

The following is a perfectly highlighted scenario as food for thought:

People who witness a crime in their neighborhood will not always give accurate information on what color clothing the criminal was wearing. For example, let's say 15 neighbors witnessed a thief breaking and entering a neighbor's home and burglarized it around 9:30 p.m. It's dark outside. How many would be able to give a complete and accurate description of what the burglar was wearing? Five out of 15 described the perpetrator as wearing all black clothing, while another five stated the perpetrator was wearing dark blue clothing. The last five said the perpetrator was wearing charcoal-colored clothing. So, which five out of the 15 gave the complete and accurate description?

I'll give you a minute to think about it…

My point exactly: YOU DON'T KNOW!

Circumstances can be a factor, such as darkness, rainy or wintry weather, heavy winds, etc. when describing what color clothes the robber wore. The focus is to apprehend the robber and bring that person to justice.

So, our focus should be on Jesus as well, giving direct attention to Him and what He has done for us; not debating, investigating, and evaluating what color robe He was wearing.

Moving along…

The Roman soldiers gave Jesus a wooden reed in His right hand then knelt on one knee before Him, still mocking Him and chanting, "Hail the King of the Jews!" They spit on Him. They struck Him with their fists. They retrieved the wooden reed from Jesus, then struck Him on the head forcibly and deliberately, causing more excruciating pain and more blood to stream down His face. Every violent hit caused the crown of thorns to further embed into His skin. The worst migraine imaginable is not comparable to the head trauma that Jesus suffered at the hands of the Roman soldiers (Matthew 27:30-31; Mark 15:18-19; John 19:3).

Jesus is then forcibly escorted to the Judgment Hall by the Roman soldiers. Just outside of the Hall is an area called "The Pavement", which was the Governor's judgment seat. Once again, Pontius Pilate presented Jesus to a mass of Jewish people to let them know he found no fault in Jesus. As Jesus walked forward, still wearing the crown of thorns and blood-stained robe (pick your color), the crowd saw His disfigured face and body from the scourging. The crowd saw Him in excruciating pain. The crowd saw the blood streaming from His head and body. The crowd saw that Jesus was physically weak and could barely stand because of the physical trauma He had suffered at the hands of the Roman torturers and soldiers. Their response was:

"CRUCIFY HIM! CRUCIFY HIM!" (John 19:5-6)

Pontius Pilate pleaded with the people for the release of Jesus, but the Sanhedrin Council and Jewish people blatantly disregarded his request. They were totally against his appeal. Since they could not prove that Christ was a threat to Caesar's government, they brought a religious accusation against Him: Christ claimed equality with God by saying He is the Son of God. To the Jews, that was considered blasphemy, which should be punishable unto death (John 19:7).

The possibility that Jesus could be the Son of God caused Pilate to be uncomfortable and more afraid (John 19:8).

Pilate took Jesus into the Judgment Hall and asked Him, "Where did you come from?" Jesus would not answer him (John 19:9). Since Jesus would not respond to Pilate's question, Pilate tried to intimidate Him by saying that as a Roman governor, "I have the power or authority to release you or crucify you" (John 19:10). Jesus calmly and quietly responded by saying, "Whatever power you possess has been given to you by God. All governments are appointed by God. And all authority, whether spiritual or civil, is from God." In other words, the power or authority Pilate possessed came from God the Father.

Scripture mentions "The one who delivered me to you." That could possibly refer to:

- ❖ Judas, the betrayer
- ❖ Caiaphas, the High Priest
- ❖ The Jewish people

The Jews should have responded differently towards Jesus. They had the scriptures which foretold the coming of the Messiah. Instead of recognizing Him, they rejected Him. Even though Pontius Pilate was guilty, Caiaphas, Judas, and the Jewish people were guiltier in punishing and killing Jesus (John 19:11).

The problem they had was that they were expecting the Messiah to conquer and overthrow their enemy — the Roman oppressors. Jesus, however, came to save ALL mankind from sin. That, my friends, is what they failed to understand.

Even after all he had witnessed for himself, Pontius Pilate was STILL convinced of Jesus' innocence and was determined to release Him. The Jews, in their argument against releasing Jesus, used a higher authority figure over Pilate by saying, "If you let this man go, you are no friend of Caesar's!" (John 19:12). (Caesar was the official title of the Roman Emperor.) In other words, Caesar was the head honcho over all the Roman people, including Pontius Pilate. Fear struck Pilate. He could not afford to have the Jews accuse him of being disloyal to Caesar! They acted as if Caesar was their king. The Jewish people of that era hated Caesar and would have loved to witness his demise and be liberated from under his authority. So, they pretended to protect Caesar's empire from the threat of Christ, who claimed to be a king.

The preparation of the Passover was about the sixth hour (noon to 3:00 p.m.). Pilate pleaded one last time for the release of Jesus by saying, "Behold your King!" The Jews' reply was, "AWAY WITH HIM! CRUCIFY HIM!" In defense of Jesus, Pilate asked, "Shall I crucify your King?" The Chief Priest said, "We have no king but Caesar" (John 19:14-15). It was then Pilate ordered the Roman soldiers to crucify Jesus (John 19:16).

Jesus was then led on foot to a place called Golgotha Hill in Jerusalem—also called Calvary—which was shaped like a bald head or skull. Jesus carried a crossbeam, which probably weighed 100 pounds. He had already suffered severe trauma and was under great distress because of the sins of humanity being transferred to Him. Jesus started out carrying the crossbeam in a tremendous state of weakness, but none of the Gospels mention Him collapsing while carrying the crossbeam to Calvary. I believe it was a difficult journey for Him to carry that heavy cross in His weak condition. Scripture says that a black man by the name Simon of Cyrene was compelled by the Roman soldiers to help Jesus bear the crossbeam to Calvary (Matthew 27:32; Mark 15:21; Luke 23:26).

There was a large number of sympathetic people weeping for Jesus as they watched Him being led by the Roman soldiers. He addressed the women in the crowd. "Daughters of Jerusalem, do not cry for me, but cry for yourselves and your children, which includes generations to come." Jesus prophesied to them about the terrible destruction that would come upon Jerusalem in A.D. 70. The suffering and sorrow of those days will be so great and so terrible that people will say it is a blessing for barren women never to conceive offspring and breastfeed them. Then, sinful man will desire greatly for the rocks of the mountains to protect them from the Romans. So, if they do these things to a green tree (He was referring to Himself), what shall happen to the dry tree (which is sinful man)? **The day of retribution is near! "The wrath of the Lamb is coming; and who shall be able to stand?" (Luke 23:27-31; Revelation 6:16-17).**

In the procession were also two malefactors with Jesus, also heading to Calvary to be crucified. Once they arrived at Calvary, the crossbeam that Jesus and Simon carried was connected to the other crossbeam that was already there laying on the ground.

Jesus was offered wine to drink, which was mixed with either sour wine or vinegar and water. After tasting it, He would not drink it (Matthew 27:34; Mark 15:23). Jesus was stripped naked and laid on the cross with His arms stretched out by the Roman soldiers. They took sharp, pointed pieces of metal spikes and nailed His hands and feet to the cross with a hammer. His body had already been through extreme torture; now they were inflicting more agonizing pain. To make matters more intensely worse, the cross was raised up by the Roman soldiers, which caused Jesus even more excruciating pain. He began experiencing difficulty breathing because of the cramping of His upper body. To breathe better and receive more oxygen to His body, Jesus would push Himself up by His feet, which brought extreme discomfort to His nailed feet. Because of the position of His outstretched arms and shoulders, for quite some time, exhaling became a major factor in trying to breathe normally.

"Then said Jesus, "Father, forgive them; for they know not what they do." And they parted His raiment and cast lots."
Luke 23:34

Jesus had no resentment, unforgiveness, nor any desire to punish:

- ❖ Judas Iscariot for betraying Him.
- ❖ The Chief Priests, Pharisees, Scribes, Elders, Officers, and the group of soldiers responsible for apprehending Him for no reason.
- ❖ Annas and his son-in-law, Caiaphas, and all of the religious leaders for their false accusations and interrogations.

- ❖ Every officer and religious leader involved in blatantly mocking Him, spitting on Him, and hitting Him.
- ❖ Pontius Pilate for giving the unnecessary command to have Him scourged.
- ❖ The Roman torturers who humiliated and tortured Him.
- ❖ Pontius Pilate for his command, out of fear, to have Him crucified—even though he knew Jesus was innocent.
- ❖ Every Roman soldier involved in crucifying Him.
- ❖ You and me for our sins that caused Him to be put to death.

The Roman soldiers divided Jesus' clothing into four pieces. His coat had no seam in it because it was made out of woven material. This kind of material was (and is) expensive but durable enough to last a long period of time. Because of that, the soldiers decided not to tear it apart and, instead, cast lots. Casting lots was the basic reason for proposing fairness and unbiased decisions on important matters. This was not considered a contest or gambling game, but more of an impartial decision on who would keep His coat.

They did not realize they had fulfilled the prophecy that said, "They part My garments among them, and cast lots upon my vesture" (Psalm 22:18).

The people were standing and looking at Jesus hanging on the cross. Also, the rulers laughed at Him as if He were stupid, declaring that since He saved others, let Him save Himself—if He be Christ, the chosen of God. The Roman soldiers also mocked Him, approaching Him with vinegar (sour wine) and declaring, "If You be the King of the Jews, save Yourself!" (Luke 23:35-37).

Pontius Pilate wrote a superscription, which was also written over Jesus in Greek, Latin, and Hebrew:

"THIS IS THE KING OF THE JEWS."
(Luke 23:38; John 19:19)

The Chief Priests did not like the superscription that Pilate wrote. They wanted him to change it to say, "I AM KING OF THE JEWS." Pilate refused to change what he had already wrote. His reply to the Chief Priests was, "What I have written shall remain" (John 19:21-22).

One of the malefactors hanging on a cross had the audacity to insult Jesus: "If you are the Christ, save Yourself and us." But the other malefactor criticized him for his demeaning remarks towards Jesus. Then, he asked him a question: "Do you even fear God? We are all suffering condemnation." In other words, they were being condemned to die. He continued, "We have received our just punishment for the crimes we committed. But this man has done nothing wrong." He then addresses Jesus: "Lord, remember me when you come into Your Kingdom" (Luke 23:39-42). Jesus responded to him in truth and assured him that day that he would be with Him in Paradise (Luke 23:43).

Where is Paradise? Jesus says, "He that hath an ear, let him hear what the Spirit saith unto the churches; to him that overcometh will I give to eat of the Tree of Life, which is in the midst of the Paradise of God" (Revelation 2:7). Jesus declares that those who are listening, let them listen to what the Spirit is communicating to the churches. Every believer who has repented and received Christ Jesus as their personal Lord and Savior, and also those who have received the precious gift of the Holy Ghost, are the blood-washed saints who have overcome the world by enduring persecutions, tribulations, and temptations for the cause of the Gospel. They will eat from the Tree of Life that is located in the middle area of the Paradise of God. Paradise is known as Heaven where God lives.

"When Jesus therefore saw His mother and the disciple standing by, whom he loved, He saith unto His mother, "Woman, behold thy son!" Then saith He to the disciple, "Behold thy mother!" And from that hour, that disciple took her unto his own home."
(John 19:26-27)

This portrait of the mother and son — viewed by Jesus — proves to us just how much God loves and values family.

Jesus purposely called His mother "Woman". Some people would have said that He was being disrespectful by talking to her that way, but He knew He had accomplished His Father's will on earth. Jesus, the Son of God the Father, who is from everlasting to everlasting, had every right to call her "Woman". Even though she was chosen and favored by God among women to give natural birth to Jesus, it was Jesus who died for her sins and gave her new life (or spiritual birth) in Him.

"It was at the ninth hour [3:00 p.m.] when Jesus cried with a loud voice, "My God, My God: Why have You forsaken Me?"
(Mark 15:34)

Jesus—who was SINLESS—took upon Himself the sins of the world. He was expressing emotion towards the abandonment of His Father in Heaven. Sin separated us from God Almighty. Sin also caused us to be enemies of God, which meant we had no peace and no fellowship with Him. God the Son was abandoned by God the Father to reconnect or bridge the gap of disconnection between God and humans through reconciliation and to plead our case as a lawyer (Romans 5:10-11; 1 John 2:1-2).

"I thirst" (John 19:28). Even though Jesus was physically thirsty in the earthly realm, He was also spiritually thirsty for souls to be harvested into the Kingdom of God. The last thirst was His longing or desire to be with His Father in Heaven.

Jesus gives living water to all who are thirsty. Everyone who consumes the water He gives is quenched of their thirst. Also, it shall be in him or her a well of water springing up into everlasting life (John 4:14).

> "When Jesus, therefore, had received the vinegar, He said, "It is finished; and He bowed His head, and gave up the ghost."
> (John 19:30)

In preparation for the Sabbath Day (Saturday), the religious leaders requested Pontius Pilate break the legs of the men hanging on the crosses to cause instantaneous death. They felt it would be improper to celebrate the Passover throughout the city of Jerusalem, which commemorated the exodus or departure of the Jewish people from Egypt—and also the death and resurrection of Jesus. The religious leaders wanted the bodies removed from their crosses so that it would not interfere with their holiday celebration. So, the Roman soldiers broke the legs of the two malefactors who had been crucified with Jesus. But when they came to Jesus, they discovered He was already dead, so His legs were not broken (John 19:31-33). One of the Roman soldiers pierced Jesus' side with his spear, causing blood and water to flow out of Him (John 19:34).

God the Son willingly died for humanity. His earthly mission was now over. The prophecies of the Old Testament in reference to the Messiah were fulfilled in Christ Jesus within the New Testament.

"Mercy, grace, salvation, the power of the Holy Ghost, healing, the blessings of Abraham, and eternal life are activated and given to all that will receive Christ Jesus as their personal Lord and Savior."
(Galatians 3:29)

Joseph of Arimathea, a secret disciple of Jesus, secretly went to Pontius Pilate for permission to take Jesus' body down from the cross for burial. Pilate granted Joseph permission, and he received help from Nicodemus, who brought a 100-pound mixture of myrrh and aloes to preserve the body from bad-smelling odors. So, they removed the body of Jesus from the cross. Myrrh and aloes were placed on His body and then wrapped in white strips of linen cloth for burial (John 19:38-40).

There was a garden tomb in Jerusalem near Calvary where no man had been laid to rest, which was prophesied by the Prophet Isaiah (John 19:41).

"And He made His grave with the wicked, and with the rich in His death because He had done no violence; neither was any deceit in His mouth" (Isaiah 53:9). The Gospel of Jesus Christ was not misleading nor was it misrepresented. When He spoke, He always spoke the truth to His disciples, audiences, and religious leaders.

Jesus was laid to rest in Joseph of Arimathea's tomb. This was a very expensive tomb that was skillfully chiseled and created for burying rich, deceased people. A great stone was placed over the entrance or doorway of the tomb where Jesus was buried. It was also sealed to keep grave robbers from entering into the tomb of Jesus (Matthew 27:60; Mark 15:46).

"After Joseph of Arimathea left the graveyard where Jesus was buried, Mary Magdalene and Mary, the mother of James, Joseph, and Salome, and the wife of Zebedee, came unto the tomb of Jesus. They were faithful to the ministry of Jesus, even when the disciples deserted Him; but these faithful women continued with Jesus to the very end."
(Matthew 27:6)

The Day of Preparation, also called the First Day of the Passover, was the day of Jesus' crucifixion. On the following day, the Chief Priests and Pharisees came together to meet with Pontius Pilate, worried about what Jesus had told them in regards to His resurrection. In response, they requested special guards be placed at the tomb of Jesus, to keep the disciples from stealing His body (Matthew 27:62-66).

CHAPTER 12: Jesus Preaches in Hell

Jesus descended into Hell to preach to the spirits in prison (1 Peter 3:19). There was a great gulf that separated Hades from Hell. In this place, the fate of the spirits was already settled.

Hades was a place for the righteous spirits, and Hell was a place for the unrighteous spirits. Between the two places, the spirits were allowed to see and communicate with one another, but not allowed to visit each other (Luke 16:23-31).

Jesus bridged the gap between the two places, meaning He preached the Gospel to both the righteous and unrighteous spirits because they had never heard the Gospel preached before during their lifetime on earth.

So, the souls that believed were saved, and Jesus led them out of captivity after His victorious resurrection. The bodies of many saints were unleashed from the grave. They traveled into the Holy City and appeared to many people (Matthew 27:52-53).

CHAPTER 13: Jesus' Resurrection

The Sabbath had already passed and the first day of the week had come. Daybreak had started, but it was still dark. Two faithful women were enroute to the tomb of Jesus, with spices they had prepared for His body. When Mary Magdalene and Mary, the wife of Zebedee, approached the tomb, they were surprised to see the large stone had been rolled away. They entered inside the tomb and discovered that the body of Jesus was missing (Matthew 28:1).

Before Mary Magdalene and Mary, the wife of Zebedee, had arrived to the tomb of Jesus, a supernatural phenomenon had taken place at the tomb of Jesus. An angel of the Lord descended from Heaven to earth and rolled back the stone from the entrance of the tomb and sat on top of it. His appearance was similar to lightning, and his clothing was white as snow. Fear gripped the keepers of the graveyard so profoundly while staring at the angel, they fell to the ground as dead men (Matthew 28:2-4).

"The angel said to the women, "Don't fear; for I know you are looking for Jesus. He is alive, just as He said. Take a look and see the place where Jesus was laid to rest. Get in a hurry; tell His disciples that He is alive from the dead. Jesus is already in Galilee, and you will see Him there. You have been informed because I have told you." So, the women departed swiftly from the graveyard with fear and great joy and did as the angel had directed them to do."
(Matthew 28:5-8).

Mary Magdalene and Mary, the wife of Zebedee, were running to bring Jesus' disciples word of His resurrection. As they went to communicate this supernatural phenomenon to the disciples, Jesus greeted them by saying, "All hail!", which is interpreted to mean "Rejoice!" They replied by falling to their knees and worshipping Him (Matthew 28:9). Jesus told them (with a word of comfort), "Be not afraid: Go, tell my brothers to meet me in Galilee. That is where they will see Me" (Matthew 28:10).

Mary Magdalene shared the good news with the disciples about Jesus, but they did not believe her and feared for their lives. Then, Jesus appeared and stood in the midst of them. He spoke a word of comfort: "Peace be unto you." Jesus then showed them his nail-scarred hands and pierced side. Joy filled the disciples' hearts, knowing that Jesus was risen from the dead—just as He said! Jesus comforts and commissions them by saying, "Peace be unto you; just as My Father had sent me, I'm now sending you." Then, he breathed on them and said, "Receive ye the Holy Ghost" (John 20:18-22).

Jesus then tells the disciples, "Whosever's sins you remit, they are remitted unto them; and whosoever's sins you retain, they are retained." In other words, once the Gospel has been preached to the audience or individual who was witnessed to, those who repent and receive Christ as Lord and Savior of their lives, the disciples were authorized to tell the people that their sins have been forgiven; for those who refuse to repent and accept Christ as Lord and Savior of their lives, the disciples must tell them that until they repent, they are still sinners. Furthermore, if those who do not repent die a physical death, they will perish forever in Hell (John 20:23).

Now, one of the disciples named Thomas was not present at the time to witness seeing Jesus risen from the dead. The 10 disciples told him that Jesus appeared unto them and showed them His nail-scarred hands and pierced side, but Thomas was disbelieving of them. He said to them, "I will believe when I see the nail-scarred hands and pierced side and touch it for myself. Then, I will believe" (John 20:24-25).

Eight days passed, and Jesus appeared to the disciples again. This time, Thomas was with them. Again, Jesus stood in the midst of them and said, "Peace be unto you." Jesus turned to Thomas—the one who doubted His resurrection—and invited him to touch His nail-scarred hands and pierced side. It is unclear whether or not Thomas took Jesus up on the offer, but Thomas was convinced and his doubting ways ceased, as was evident when he said to Jesus, "My Lord and my God." Jesus said to Thomas, "You believe me because you see me. Blessed are they that have not seen me and believe" (John 20:26-29).

Peter decided to go fishing and the other disciples were in agreement. They went to the Sea of Tiberias at nighttime to catch fish but caught nothing. When morning came, Jesus was standing on the shore, but the disciples did not recognize Him. So, He yelled aloud to them, "Children, do you have any meat?" The disciples responded, "No." Jesus then advised the disciples to throw their nets on the right side of the ship. So, they took heed to the word that was given to them and dropped their nets on the right side of the ship—and received a great load of fish! One hundred fifty-three fish were caught, and the added miracle was that their nets did not break under the weight of the load! John, the beloved of Jesus, told Peter that the man on the shore was the Lord. When Peter heard that, he hurried and put on his clothes because he was naked. The ships were then pulled up to the shore of the Sea of Galilee. This was the third time Jesus appeared to the disciples, and He prepared fish and bread for them to eat for breakfast. Jesus gave thanks for the food, and they all ate breakfast together (John 21:2-14).

After breakfast, Jesus had a talk with Simon Peter, the one who denied Him before His death. Jesus confronted Simon about the denial in a loving way. The first question that was asked to Peter was, "Do you love Me more than these?" (This could have meant His fellow colleagues (the disciples) or His occupation as a fisherman or both.) Peter replied, "Yes, Lord. You know that I love You." Jesus replied, "Feed my sheep." Jesus then questioned Peter a second time: "Do you love Me?" Peter again replied "Yes, Lord. You know that I love You." Jesus again stated, "Feed my sheep." Jesus posed the question a third time: "Do you love Me?" Peter felt sad when Jesus asked that third time. I'm sure he felt remorseful for denying Jesus three times previously. Peter's reply this time was: "Lord, You know all things: You know that I love You." Jesus told him, "Feed my sheep." Then, Jesus foretold Peter's death: "When you were a young man, you had freedom to go wherever you wanted to go. But as an elderly man, you will be apprehended, constrained, and carried off to be executed." Scripture tells us that Peter would glorify God by dying as a martyr (John 21:15-19).

Jesus then gives final instructions to the disciples: Carry out the Great Commission at hand. Jesus commissioned the disciples to preach the Gospel to everyone. The ultimate objective of the Savior's plan in the earthly realm is world evangelism and that souls would be harvested into the Kingdom of God. Two results will occur from the Great Commission: Those who believe will be saved and baptized AND those who do not believe will be condemned (Mark 16:15-16).

> "And these signs shall follow them that believe; in My name shall they cast out devils; they shall speak with new tongues; they shall take up serpents; and if they drink any deadly thing, it shall not hurt them; they shall lay hands on the sick and they shall recover."
> (Mark 16:17-18).

The 40th day since Jesus' resurrection had come (Acts 1:3). Jesus and the disciples were gathered at the Mount called Olivet. Jesus told them, "You shall receive power after the Holy Ghost has come on you; and you will represent Me in Jerusalem, Judea, Samaria, and to the ends of the earth." After He finished speaking, the disciples watched as He ascended and disappeared into the clouds. As they continued to look towards Heaven, two angels in white attire appearing as men addressed the disciples: "Men of Galilee: Why are you standing and looking up toward Heaven? This same Jesus, which ascended into Heaven, will return to earth in similar manner" (Acts 1:8-11).

The disciples departed on the Sabbath day from the Mount called Olivet and traveled back to Jerusalem, which was about three-quarters of a mile away. Once they returned to Jerusalem, they went up to a room called the Upper Room. Altogether, there was a total of 120 disciples on one accord, praying and making their petitions known unto God while waiting on the promise of the Comforter to come (Acts 1:12-15).

CHAPTER 14: SPECIAL NOTE

NO ONE knows the day nor the hour when the Son of Man will return. This is in regards to the Son of God's second advent or second coming. NO MAN knows, nor the angels in Heaven, nor the Son; ONLY God the Father in Heaven knows the time. While in His human form on earth, Jesus did not mention any details about His second coming because the information was not revealed to Him by His Father in Heaven. Yes, he was all-knowing while on earth. As a matter-of-fact, He knew everything about every person. Remember: He was 100% deity as the Son of God, but also 100% human as the Son of Man. Now, He sits at the right hand of the Father. NOW, God the Son knows when He shall return. Why? Because God the Father and God the Son are ONE!

GOD THE HOLY GHOST

Clarence Jordan, Jr.

CHAPTER 15: God the Holy Ghost

God the Holy Ghost — also known as the Holy Spirit — is the third person of the Godhead, which proceeds from God the Father and God the Son. The third person of the Blessed Trinity resembles the Father and the Son, equal in power and glory, united with the Father and the Son to be worshipped, to have faith in, and to be obeyed.

The Holy Ghost is also known by other names and titles, such as:

1. **Author of Holy Scriptures**
2. **Comforter**
3. **Spirit of Truth**
4. **Sealer**
5. **Revealer**
6. **Indweller of Believers**
7. **Spirit of Life**
8. **Teacher**

Clarence Jordan, Jr.

THE HOLY GHOST AS THE AUTHOR OF HOLY SCRIPTURES

All 66 books of the Bible—from Genesis to Revelation—were written, inspired, and revealed to the writers of the Scriptures by the "Breath of God": The Holy Ghost. Each writer received impartation of what to write in a supernatural way. No prophecy of scriptures in the Bible was formulated by man's personal interpretation or intelligence: ONLY by the inspiration of God. Each individual's penmanship of the Old Testament writings, as well as the New Testament writings, was authorized by the Holy Spirit. The Holy Scriptures are profitable or beneficial to every inheritor of salvation. It is also profitable for doctrine, for rebuke, for correction, and for instruction in righteousness (2 Timothy 3:15-16).

Blessed Trinity

THE HOLY GHOST AS THE COMFORTER

Jesus, by His miraculous, supernatural power, comforted and cured many people who were lame, blind, mute, maimed, deaf, sick, diseased, and under demonic possession (Psalm 34:19; Matthew 15:30-31).

Also, Jesus (who was rich, but for our personal benefit became poor), through His poverty, we might become in this present age and in the age to come rich (2 Corinthians 8:9).

Jesus revealed to the disciples that He will pray to God the Father, and He will send another Comforter, which is the Holy Ghost. And God the Father will send the Comforter in Jesus' name (John 14:16,26).

Jesus turned water into wine at a wedding reception (John 2:1-11).

Jesus supernaturally used a little boy's lunch to feed 5,000 people with two small fishes and five loaves of bread (John 6:6-13).

Jesus supernaturally resurrected Lazarus from the dead by calling his name from the tomb where he laid (John 11:38-44).

Clarence Jordan, Jr.

THE HOLY GHOST AS THE SPIRIT OF TRUTH

The Spirit of Truth, also known as the Holy Ghost, will teach the truth and glorify Jesus, who is the Living Word and the Living Truth. When the Spirit of Truth comes, He will lead or direct and advise the Spirit-filled saint into all truth through the written Word and revelation of God.

The Holy Ghost will only convey the things which God the Father and God the Son desires to communicate with the church or an individual. The Holy Ghost will never speak of Himself (John 16:13-15). God's Word that is spoken out of the mouth of His Messenger will never return void, but achieved or accomplished by God's purposeful and masterful plan (Isaiah 55:11).

THE HOLY GHOST AS THE SEALER

Every believer who has been empowered by the precious gift of the Holy Ghost are those who have repented of their sins and accepted Jesus Christ as their personal Lord and Savior. The Holy Ghost seals every believer as God's sons and daughters. The Holy Ghost is the promise of our inheritance.

Every saint of God is sealed with the Holy Ghost as a sign that we belong to God until the Day of Redemption. The Day of Redemption refers to the future state of our resurrected or glorified body that we shall receive in Heaven. Our bodies will be transformed from corruptible to incorruptible, and from mortal to immortality. This "earth suit" — our human flesh — is prone to sickness, disease, injuries, aging, death, and decay. This came about through the sin of Adam (Genesis 3:2-7). God breathed into Adam's nostrils the breath of life, and he became a living human being (Genesis 2:7). Because of the first Adam, the nature of all human beings became sinfully and mortally corrupted.

HOWEVER, the Second Adam, which is Jesus, became a quickening Spirit. He is the Life-Giver or the One who gives eternal life to all believers who believe in Him (1 Corinthians 15:22).

When the resounding trumpet of the Son of God sounds, the dead in Christ (the corruptible) shall be transformed incorruptible first. And those who are still alive shall be transformed from mortal to immortality (1 Corinthians 15:51-54; 1 Thessalonians 4:14-18).

Clarence Jordan, Jr.

THE HOLY GHOST AS THE REVEALER

The Holy Ghost (or Holy Spirit) is the Revealer of mysteries, prophecies, visions, and dreams.

The mystery of God is revealed by the teaching, preaching, and witnessing of the Gospel of Jesus Christ to lost souls by warning them of the future judgment of God—and to build up and admonish the new converts by all wisdom of the Word of God unto perfection in Christ Jesus (Colossians 1:28).

God revealed to the Prophet Joel His Spirit being poured out on all flesh. Sons and daughters will prophesy. Elderly men will dream dreams. Young men will see visions. It shall also be poured upon men and women servants. God promised to pour out His Spirit in the future. He also promised to show wonders in the Heavens and on the earth—in other words, the unexplainable, supernatural phenomenon of God (Joel 2:28-30).

On the Day of Pentecost—the 50th day after the resurrection of Jesus Christ—the Holy Ghost fell on all 12 disciples PLUS on the 108 persons present in the Upper Room. This was just the beginning of the manifestation of the prophecy of the Holy Ghost being fulfilled, which was prophesied by the Prophet Joel in the Old Testament (Acts 2:4). Peter made reference to this prophecy to the men of Judea and all who were there in Jerusalem (Acts 2:16-20).

Blessed Trinity

THE HOLY GHOST AS THE INDWELLER OF BELIEVERS

Not only is the Holy Ghost WITH us, He is also IN us — fulfilling the purpose and plan of God for the Kingdom of God's Gospel, which Jesus preached about (Mark 1:14-15; Luke 4:43).

The Holy Ghost empowers and equips every believer for winning lost souls into the Kingdom of God. Preaching, teaching, witnessing, and evangelizing cannot be accomplished by our own efforts; only by the power of the Holy Ghost. Any church that is powerless or lacking spiritual power is ineffective for ministry.

Jesus proclaimed to the audience in the synagogue that the Spirit of the Lord is on Him; reason being, He has been anointed to speak to human conditions, such as:

- ❖ **Deficiency: To preach the Gospel to the poor.**
- ❖ **Sadness: To heal the brokenhearted.**
- ❖ **Sin: To proclaim freedom to the captives.**
- ❖ **Affliction: Recover of sight to the blind (for example).**
- ❖ **Despair: To set at liberty those who are oppressed.**
- ❖ **Salvation: To preach the acceptable year of the Lord (Luke 4:18-19).**

It's the anointing that destroys the yoke and removes every burden (Isaiah 10:27).

Clarence Jordan, Jr.

The anointing and power of the Holy Ghost that was operating in Peter's life caused a man who was born crippled and a beggar to be supernaturally healed (Acts 3:1-7).

The shadow of Peter healed multitudes of people who were sick in Jerusalem in the streets, laid on beds and couches. Also, those with unclean spirits were cast out miraculously by the power and anointing of the Holy Ghost (Acts 5:15-16).

Philip (a Deacon/Evangelist full of the Holy Ghost) traveled to Samaria, preaching Christ unto the people there. Many miraculous miracles were demonstrated by the power of the Holy Ghost operating through Philip. Unclean spirits were cast out of many who were possessed, and the paralyzed and lame were supernaturally healed (Acts 8:5-7).

As Peter was preaching to Cornelius and all who were present in his house, the Holy Ghost fell on each of them as they heard the Word of God. They began to speak in another language and glorify God (Acts 10:34-46).

Paul witnessed to the men at Ephesus, and they accepted Jesus as their Lord and Savior. Paul laid hands on each of the 12 men and they received the Holy Ghost, spoke in another language and prophesied (Acts 19:1-7).

God performed extraordinary miracles through Paul. Even the handkerchiefs and aprons that touched him were given to the sick, and their sicknesses were supernaturally healed and the evil spirits departed from them (Acts 19:11-12).

THE HOLY GHOST AS THE SPIRIT OF LIFE

There is no judgment on anyone who has accepted Christ Jesus as their Lord and Savior. Through the redeeming work of Christ on the cross, the law of the Spirit of Life has released every believer from the law of sin and death. The law was unable to produce holiness or pure life from sin because it was powerless through the flesh (Romans 8:1-3). Simply observing the law could not save anyone. The law was a ministry of condemnation. In other words, if you committed any sin worthy of death, there was no mercy or grace to release you from the curse of the law.

Christ became a curse for us by redeeming us from the curse of the law by hanging on the cross and shedding His own blood for our justification. Only the just shall live by faith! (Galatians 3:10-13)

As you study God's Word, the Holy Spirit will help prepare and enable you—to the best of your ability—with excellence, presenting yourself to God approved or acceptable, a workman who is unashamed, accurately, carefully, and skillfully preaching or teaching the Word of Truth. It is an AWESOME responsibility or task that should never be taken lightly (2 Timothy 2:15).

Clarence Jordan, Jr.

THE HOLY GHOST AS THE TEACHER

"The Comforter, which is the Holy Ghost, whom the Father will send in Jesus' name, will teach you all things, and bring all things to your remembrance."
(John 14:25)

As a citizen of the Kingdom of God, we must allow the Holy Ghost to teach us as we read, study, and meditate on God's written Word. We should prayerfully ask for knowledge when there is something in His Word we don't understand. The Book of the Law or the Word of God should never depart out of our mouth; but we must reflect on it day and night, that we may adhere or pay special attention to do all that is written in the Bible: just as Joshua was commanded to do by God, concerning the Book of the Law. It is then we will make our way prosperous and have good success (Joshua 1:7-8).

Jesus used a parable of the sower who went out to sow to illustrate His message to the audience that was present with Him. Now, when the audience had departed, the 12 disciples inquired about the parable of the sower. Jesus told them, "The secret of the Kingdom of God has been granted to you. But to those that are unsaved, everything is told in parables so that the unsaved may be always seeing but never perceiving (comprehend), always hearing but never understanding; unless they repent and be saved (Mark 4:2-20).

CHAPTER 16: FIVE SYMBOLS OF THE HOLY GHOST

DOVE

After John the Baptist baptized Jesus in the Jordan River, John saw in the realm of the spirit the Heavens open and the Holy Ghost descending as a dove and glorious light, shining on the Son of God (Mathew 3:16; Mark 1:10; John 1:32).

A dove represents peace and meekness. These are just two out of the nine distinctive characteristics of the Fruits of the Spirit that every Spirit-filled believer should maintain and exemplify on a daily basis (Galatians 5:22).

FIRE

John the Baptist preached to his audience that he only baptized them with water unto repentance—in other words, those who have made a decision to change their mind and feel remorseful or godly sorrowful for the sins they have committed against God unto a changed life. John also mentioned, "He [the Messiah] who is coming after me is mightier than I, whose sandals I'm not worthy to remove; He shall baptize you with the Holy Ghost and with fire" (Matthew 3:11).

Fire refines gold by consuming all impurities so that it will become pure gold. The Holy Ghost is like fire: It consumes all sins and gives us a victorious life of holiness in this present age.

Fire can also mean judgment upon those who are unrepentant and have not accepted Jesus as their personal Savior. They will, in the future, be cast into Hell and suffer torment at the hands of demons, as well as suffer unquenchable, burning fire…continuously…non-stop…THROUGHOUT ALL ETERNITY!!!

OIL

We are anointed by the Holy One, Jesus Christ, in which the Holy Ghost was sent in His name by God the Father (John 14:26; 1 John 2:20). The Holy Ghost enables every Spirit-filled saint to perceive the truth. The Holy Spirit will also enlighten our minds to understand the Word of God. We must study to present ourselves to God, approved a workman (tested by trial) who has no reason to be ashamed, accurately handling and skillfully teaching the Word of Truth (2 Timothy 2:15).

Just as Peter was allowed to walk on water by the word of Jesus, we, through the anointing and power of the Holy Ghost, can do exactly what Jesus did when He was on the earth. Jesus also said we will perform even greater works than He did, because His work on earth is complete. He has already returned back to Heaven and is seated at the right hand of God the Father (John 14:12). Jesus is tremendously greater than we are. He is the Son of God! There are many more miracles that He performed that are not recorded in the Bible. Today, we have technology at our disposal that was not around during the age of Jesus. We can win many people to Christ through phones, radio, television, internet, and social media.

WATER

Water baptism is the believer's outwardly sign of identification with Christ's death, burial, and resurrection. We now can walk in the newness of life because we have forsaken or deserted our sinful ways. We are unified with Christ's death and burial (by being submerged in water) and unified with His resurrection (by being raised out of the water) (Romans 6:3-6).

Just as water is purified from pollution or contamination, the Holy Ghost purifies believers from polluted and contaminated affections, thoughts, desires, and actions.

Jesus stood, and with a loud voice said, "If any man is thirsty, let him come to Me and drink. Anyone who believes in Me (who adheres to, trusts in, and relies on Me), as the scripture has said, 'From His innermost being will flow continually rivers of Living Water'..."(John 7:37-38).

Jesus was speaking of the Holy Ghost, which those who believed in Him (as Savior) were to receive afterward. The Spirit had not yet been given because Jesus was not yet glorified (raised to honor) (John 7:39). In other words, His mission on earth was not complete until He had died for the sins of humanity, been resurrected from the dead, ascended back to Heaven, and then seated at the right hand of God the Father.

WIND

Jesus illustrated His point to Nicodemus, a Pharisee, by using the wind as an example of the work of the Holy Ghost. The wind blows where it desires. The Holy Ghost works sovereignly in that same way.

There is no one on the face of the planet earth who can visibly see or know the origin and destination of the wind, but everyone knows that it exists. The same is true of the Holy Ghost. We are unable to touch the wind, but we are able to feel it. This, too, is similar in regards to the Holy Ghost (John 3:8).

CONCLUSION

I encourage all believers who have not been filled with the Holy Ghost to seek for it. Those who persistently ask receive; and anyone who keeps persistently seeking finds; and to anyone who keeps persistently knocking, the door will be opened.

"If the son asks his father for a fish, would he give him a snake? Or if he asked for an egg, would his father give him a scorpion? If you (who are sinful by nature) know how to give good gifts to your children, how much more will your Heavenly Father give the Holy Ghost to those who ask and continue to ask Him!"
(Luke 11-9-13)

With great power comes great responsibility. To all who have been given much, much is required (Luke 12:48). As servants of the Most High God, we have been empowered and commissioned to win the world to Christ.

Clarence Jordan, Jr.

INVITATION TO CHRISTIAN DISCIPLESHIP

I extend an invitation to those of you who have not accepted Jesus Christ as your personal Savior. I want you to know that God's love for you is unconditional, inexpressible, and incredible. God the Father proved His love for you by sending His Only Begotten Son to save you from your sins. Jesus loved you so much that He was willing to disrobe Himself from His throne in Heaven by stepping out of eternity and into time, taking on the form of man to destroy the works of Satan who is the originator of sin (1 John 3:8). Christ also came to save you from your sins by suffering and dying on a cross—a punishment He did not deserve. Why, then, did He do it? Because YOU were worth it! YOU are the apple of God's eye. YOU are very precious to Him. God loves you with an everlasting love that will never end. You can come as you are to the throne of God. I don't care what you've done. Jesus has already paid for it with His own blood over 2,000 years ago. It does not matter what country you live in. God can save you right now, right where you are. Salvation is available to you.

If you feel something tugging in the pit of your belly right now; if you feel a stirring in your heart, mind, and soul…let me share with you what that is:

It is the presence of Almighty God calling you unto repentance. Right where you sit, raise your hands unto the Lord and repeat the following words:

Lord Jesus, come into my life and save me from my sins. I believe that you died on the cross just for me and that God the Father raised you from the dead. I thank You right now for saving me. My life from this day forward will never be the same.

In Jesus' name I pray, Amen.

My dear brother or sister, WELCOME to the family of God! You are now a Kingdom citizen. I encourage you to find a Bible-believing church where you can be fed the Word of God and grow spiritually. I also encourage you to seek for the precious gift of the Holy Ghost so that you, too, can win lost souls for Christ (Acts 1:8, 2:4).

God Bless!

Your Brother-in-Christ,
Clarence Jordan, Jr.

1 JOHN 1:9 - JOURNALING

"If we confess our sins, He is faithful and just to forgive us our sins, and to cleanse us from all unrighteousness."

The Greek word for "confess" is *homologeo*, which means "to agree with." When the Holy Spirit convicts your inner-man or spirit-being of your sins, you must immediately come into agreement with Him. No excuses will be tolerated because all excuses were nailed to the cross of Jesus. There is no sin greater than another sin. Sin is sin! Sin is what separated us from God the Father. The Father's plan for redemption had to be paid in blood by the Redeemer so that the redeemed could live again and become citizens of the Kingdom of God.

TO GOD BE THE GLORY FOR HIS SON JESUS CHRIST, OUR LORD AND SAVIOR, REDEEMER, AND MEDIATOR!

Use the following pages to make note of the times you feel convicted by the Holy Spirit for a sin you have committed; then, ask for forgiveness for that sin. Repent and be free from the chain that bound you to that sin!

"He will again have compassion on us and will subdue our iniquities. You will cast all our sins into the depths of the sea."

Micah 7:19

Blessed Trinity

Clarence Jordan, Jr.

Blessed Trinity

Clarence Jordan, Jr.

Blessed Trinity

Clarence Jordan, Jr.

Blessed Trinity

Clarence Jordan, Jr.

CLOSING PRAYER

Dear Heavenly Father,

In the precious name of Jesus. Creator of all things in Heaven and in earth. We bless Your Holy name. We pray that Your Kingdom come and Your will be done on earth, as it is in Heaven. We ask You to forgive us our sins, as we forgive those who have done us wrong. Father God, we thank You for Your Dear Son, Jesus, who died in our place on the cross for our sins.

Jesus, thank You for the gift of salvation, which you purchased with Your own blood. Thank you, Dear Jesus, for the precious gift of the Holy Ghost, which enables and anoints us to supernaturally drive out devils, heal the sick, raise the dead, open blinded eyes, and make the dumb to talk, the lame to walk, the maimed to be made whole and, most importantly, souls set free from Satan's power. We thank You for every pastor in the body of Christ who is preaching Your Word under the anointing of the Holy Ghost. We thank You for every vision that has come to pass and impacted many lives, for without a vision, the people perish. We pray that You will unify the body of Christ as one, just as You and the Father are One.

We come against every attack of Satan and the kingdom of darkness because the blood of Jesus prevails against them now — above the earth, on the earth, and under the sea. We break every stronghold of the enemy right now over every government, country, church, and family. We destroy every curse of the enemy now in the lives of Your people, by the blood of Jesus. The blood of Jesus prevails over every plan and deception of Satan. Satan, you are defeated and God Almighty is exalted.

We pray for the peace of Jerusalem that You, Father God, would bless and protect them. We pray Your blessings and protection upon our lives as well. We pray for the leadership of every country in the world. We also pray for leadership of our judicial branch, the president, legislators, senators, governors, mayors, and city council members. We pray that every decision made by these leaders would be directed by You and that we may live a quiet and peaceful life.

Father God, all the glory belongs to You for blessing me to write this book about You. I also pray Your blessings upon the publisher and publication of this book. I pray that this will be a tool to win the lost to Christ and an encouragement to the body of Christ.

In Jesus' most excellent name I pray,

Amen.

Clarence Jordan, Jr.

www.ingramcontent.com/pod-product-compliance
Lightning Source LLC
Chambersburg PA
CBHW071530080526
44588CB00011B/1619